Remote Fishing
and Sassafras Tea

Remote Fishing and Sassafras Tea

Poems

by

Carla Maria Stout

BRIGHT
HORSE
BOOKS

Copyright © 2017 by Carla Maria Stout
All rights reserved.
Printed in the United States of America

Brighthorse Books
13202 North River Drive
Omaha, NE 68112

ISBN: 978-1-944467-06-7

Cover art: Christopher Stout
Author Photo: Christopher Stout

For permission to reproduce selections from this book and for more information about Brighthorse Books and the Brighthorse Prize, visit us on the web at brighthorsebooks.com.

Brighthorse books are distributed to the trade through Ingram Book Group and its distribution partners. For more information, go to https://ipage.ingramcontent.com/ipage/li001.jsp.

To
Randy—grace, guide, gears
Christopher—sunshine through dark trees
Darian—moonlight on deepest lakes

Contents

Remote Fishing I
    (Reflections Upon a Visit to the Black Hills)   11
After Lights Was Out   15
Tricking Tosca   16
Mozart and Koi II   17
Amens and Everclear   18
Intimation of Eve   19
Hyde   20
Monsters and Genius   21
Gentle, Gentle (an elegy)   23
Baroque (after a Renaissance exhibit)   25
Harris' Sparrow   27
Pale Ride   28
Wormholes, Vivaldi and Iris   29
Dear Picasso   30
Talk Me Down   32
Cold Lies on Hot Jupiters   33
Crows in a Cornfield   34
Handle with Care   36
Dr. Marvel's Magical Medicinals   37
Flat Out Doing Sixty   39
Dog Star Rising   41
Without a Net   43
Looking Glass Menagerie   45
Road Undertaken   47
Crow   49
Heart of MCG-8-22-15
    (Art and Science of Black Stars and Blue Poets)   50
Thursdays on Meadow Road   51
Branta Canadensis   52
Seasons and Memory   53
Cathartes aura-Turkey Vulture   55

Friday Night Shift   57
Jekyll   58
Apple Pie   59
Lemon Europa   61
Roma Hands   62
Summer Whites   64
Last Call Bar and Dance Hall   65
Windflower Farm   66
Golden Eagle   68
Briar Patch   69
Remote Fishing III
    (Reflections Upon a Visit to the Black Hills)   71
About the Author   81

Remote Fishing I
(Reflections Upon a Visit to the Black Hills)

We hardly make camp while sunshine
gropes through smoky clouds, prompting
you to follow schools of fish. The cold tutors
me, holds me back so I must track
you virtually. I am too close
to write you. Paces, days and now,
silver fishes take you away so that I am
always at some safe distance. I can
still sense you remotely, so I trail along
and go remote fishing with you.

You have already crossed
many bridges to get here,
all of these taking you farther
away. How few the steps
from crawling to walking,
walking to running, running
to flying. From flying to soaring,
to subliming the very bridges
you cross.

Between the trees I know
you are up there, somewhere
on that crumbling mountain
pebbling the lake
but I don't worry
for granite and hope
only erode over epochs.

A bed of rocky coals could not keep

me away from you. I would bridge
it, traverse it, finesse it, crawl
over it in nitroglycerin gown
and immolate for you are
my seven-percent solution, my acute
fix. Only your word keeps me away.

Poised on that rock, perched over
Legion Lake, you could
hardly help sprouting wings and flying
into that mirror of blue pearl below.
Is this what heaven is? A watery
reflection of what we perceive as most deep,
most unreachable, most unfathomable.

How do you become one with granite
and clouds below? How easy you
make it look to lure and hook digits
of spruce, fronds of cirrus, three-ring
fish and low flying midnight wishes.
Is it in the strength of your untried
arms or unstudied charms?

"Sorry, little buddy," you apologize
though you grin through your regret
while your brother still curses
scaled vertebrates. "You mother,"
he says to one that gets away,
"Bring me your grandfather." You just
smile and cut your line.
The glow of you here blinds

me so I must put on psychic
shades. In the shadows on the floor,
I see the dust of your footprints
and in the mirror at the door, I see
a waning version of your smile.
Through the cabin's open window,
I hear the wind spy through trees,
sensing my secret thoughts, how the sun
couldn't shadow your smile, nor birds
rival your harvest song.

Legions of stars fence with the cage
of darkness and I regret not knowing
them all by name and rank when you
ask for them beyond Sirius and ones
which fall into our wild fantasy
to be counted like black pearls.
Ducks, nighthawks, bats and bison,
still *en garde*, count ancient lights
and breathe glitter air with us.

Only a trace of day left
when night erases our ambitions,
our inhibitions. Sky scorched,
trees are torches which fire
our tallest tales of the fish,
the tatonka and things never
sensed back home. This
is our last night and we still dream,
fish, dream remotely, too far away.
We break camp taking more

than we brought somehow,
but no heavier than mica,
than smiles, songs, thoughts
to pack. Anointing ourselves
with holy dust, we will leave
a trail for others to follow
our little caravan. And we
will be pressed close with each
other for long hours, though
our thoughts may be, even now,
as remote as the sun and other
stars, as lonesome and wandering
as the French Creek.

After Lights Was Out

The sky is gray as liver and onions
in a cast iron pan while I roll up
my mattress fast as can be. They say

it'll sleet today topping off eight inches
of heavy snow in what my buddy, Leo,
slept so late he never woke up. I don't know

where they laid him but I'm goddam sure
it were the cold that killed him. Long after
lights was out, I played him the only song I

knowed, "Plastic Jesus," on the harmonica
and they was all buzzing 'bout Leo in the library,
not listening to a word I say, "By God, the birds is back

today." You can send your sorrows to the bus
stop at Thirteenth and State where me and Leo
live in cardboard boxes warped with ice, where buses

will splash you but they ain't never late. Windows
at the library is all steamed up. Guess it's all
that heavy breathing over Dante, Shakespeare

and *National Geographic*, Leo's favorite, like
his size twelve rubber boots I make fit
with crumpled newspaper. It's sleeting now,
but hell, Leo, by God, the birds is back.

Tricking Tosca

Hey, man, check it out. Been
on the streets since I was fourteen
and I still got my strut. Come closer,
take a look. Fine as bone china
in overdrive. I ain't so worse
for the wear, not a dime over thirty,
fucking fifteen, standing here
on the corner of sixteen and Gold
by trees that look fake, stuck
in cement. But they shed in fall
and bloom in spring
like me, so maybe they's real,
too. The johns, sometimes get
rough, but they ain't all bad. 'Specially
when the opera comes. They come
in their cashmere coats and silk
scarves, in leather seats, smelling
of Armani, veal scaloppini
and fear. For Tosca and Carmen,
'specially, I dress up in my black
Mongolian fur and remember me,
in the dark, watching mama
dress up in short skirts, tall
boots, gives her "lover boy" a smoky
lullaby and whiskey-smeared,
Red Raven kiss good-bye. From
my corner, I shiver but feel the heat
of these songs. I could sing like
the birds in Tosca. I could dance
like the Gypsies in Carmen. Could be
tomorrow, I'll get my break. For tonight
just let me in, dude.

Mozart and Koi II

Mozart's No. 40 plays in the kitchen
next to the open window, while she sweeps
the floor of bittersweet. No leaves blow in,
yet green and holding tight to clear sky, which leaps
before sunrise eyes, while the andante
chases light with dark. She sweeps sunlight
at the door where I hear the pond grumble this day
which looms too soon. She could put up a fight
like the flight of geese heading west, the new sugar maple
still a fresh bouquet, but who can ignore frost reports.
She knows it isn't easy for me since the crystal
waters hide away my prey and four-strokes court
me on this day which comes too soon. In that G-minor din
she calls out but turns her back, the day I bring the fish in.

Amens and Everclear

Everyone's always trying to fix
me with their amens and their therapy
but I ain't broken, on my knees,
or even looking for a hobby.
I'm just hanging here in the alley
with eyes that don't see quite
right, my ninety-proof brain on ice,
just pissing away bad memories.
"Spare change, mister."
Yeah, I'm sweating here in May
while I play backdoor man on the patio
of the whine and concubine café,
just sweating and blowing smoke
up the skirts at their reserve tables,
served with endive and brie.
When you see their fine ankles
chained in gold and strapped in kid,
don't it just give second-hand smoke
a whole new meaning? 'Course
they say I am self-contained.
I chew on the butt of a smoke thinking,
some joke. Yeah, like a mine in an oil
spill. Christ, it's been like that since she
threw me out like a three-legged cat
in heat on a Sunday night and now
I got this fever that won't go away
lest I put it out with Everclear.
She'd always bitch that only poets is free
but damned if there ain't no one freer than me.

Intimation of Eve

Stars exhausted of all light, he still sleeps
while sunrise rushes in my blood, a cosmic
brew of knowing/unknowing. He has named
all the visible by day. Of darkness and light,
I name the invisible, infrared/ultraviolet.

This crucible of iridium upon which I creep
blanches with disinterest and fitful sleep. It burns
with the Other and I want to know the Other's name.
I stalk arbors and groves and gather the ecstasy
of wonder. Just what do we get for a name? I tire
of rooted things and would walk skies, drinking
them like water.

I want to dismember the stars, the soaring wing,
to know their workings and failings, to know
pain, the underside of things. I hunger to know
the makings of being undone.

Though He may rest, I do not, incising scaly genius
in my sleep. Must I mate intention, these incestuous
comets, while my brother breeds aimlessly? I seek
to divine the solution to this grand equation.
I have everything I need. Will I have everything
I want? Where lies this unholy creature I name?
I pace this taking down.

Hyde

Nightfall flushes whorls of breakneck bats.
Over pavers crawl blackest rats. I am free.
For now and forever I embrace the fog
and insipid air, spinning with abandon beneath
milky lamplight and inky sky. He says we
are two, but a dram of this, a pinch of salts
and it is I alone who dances beneath moon's
menacing grin, where I'll never sleep. All's not
for evil. I live to live, not live to thrive.

Too long caged, I come out panting. Oh these
porcelain whores on red velvet who set fire
to my lips. My hands about their cameo throats,
about a snifter of brandy, a weedy cigar. I massage
the base of their downy skulls, the silk of stockings,
their satin garters and they assuage the howl,
the hunger I can't name. I'll romance them
to their bleakest hour, rapture of their little deaths.

Before this night is over, I'll swoon poppies in smoky
dens, hear every moan and whisper, feel earth's
wobble, burn of every hell-bent star. This blood
rushes with every leap and gasp I take. I stomp off
my wounds, each heavenly body.

Far away from day, roosters alarm and sparrows
riddle the runaway gray. A knife of sunlight slashes
through bricks and vision's thieves, carving up
remains of night. Once again I resign myself
to a vial in the apothecary. Fear tomorrow
when every shadow will harbor only me.

Monsters and Genius

That monsters and genius
come in such tiny seeds,
I think when I read lines
in Jackson and Perkins 'cause
raising roses is all about sex
and gratuitous politics
anyway. What beauty
the rose that madness
and sorrow can breed, I
study in the outlaw lines
of Black Magic. No amount
of wilt, rust, or thorns
can take out the magic
for me. Wonder
is blue as the loft beyond
my fingers and what I don't
know is a rumble of gray
matter and clouds between
us. The earth is a red, hot
slurry which rushes and shushes
beneath my feet, taking me
from time zone to time zone
without giving me the time
of day. And monsters are
cloned of deadly nightshade,
dark stars, stuff of nightmare
walk, shattered genome fallout
and demolition dust. And genius
is cloned of red tripled rose,
stuff of time-warp beats,
sight cheating sight, ragged

and tattered neurons tearing
at the speed of light. And both
are lost in time and out of season.

Gentle, Gentle
(an elegy)

gentle, gentle over these holy
bones of silica and sand,
no relic to time or hurtled stone,
while they, disarticulated, glowing,
lay upon this shallow
bed of friable ground.

whisper, whisper to malleus, incus
and stapes those last hallowed tones,
to fall like trees in lone, deaf woods,
to fly like sleet in fevered Winter,
to ply with feathered scepter of wordy conspire,
to plead and confess, "Stars, hide your fires . . ."

channel, channel shuttered windows
fenestrated with broken light,
hazy with layers of lichens and moss,
now cloudy to this Anatomy 102,
shaded and screened to dust and flare,
yet wide open still to gray matter stuff.

hover, hover over this rumored heart
and count its numbered murmurs,
splintering with joy's dual sides,
cajoling ecstasy where birds etch sky,
purple with pain, fruited with passion,
erratic, pulsing, arrested with solitude.

release, release this ghost of solemn
intention, mind's vagabond, well-meaning,
mixed-meaning will, potion of volition,

of poppies, sage, rose madder and thyme.
remember, remember music never played,
words never said, dreams which never fade.

Baroque
(after a Renaissance exhibit)

Do not paint me
when I am old and crafty
but paint me when I'm
young and stupid
in the throes of ecstasy.
Let Caravaggio paint
me when we are both
twenty-two for only
he can bind the pain
and the bliss of
St. Francis of Assisi.
Still what do I,
at that age, know
of pain or ecstasy. Paint
me by fire, in red,
with a glow of white
around my head. Oh,
throw me to the dragon
of St. George who is still
hungry after two lambs
a day. By fire, to a dragon
who never eats his dinner
rare. Paint me, Leal, for I
am vain. Mark me
with your skulls
and your crowns. On
judgment day, send
cherubs to blow bubbles
over my bones, stacks
of books, snuffed out candles,
unturned games and Dorian

looks. Remember
me on a cloudy day. Paint
me black and blue
and forget my name.

Harris' Sparrow

No corruption of time, brown
and leafless days grow shorter.
This gnawing hunger is all that fills
my belly. Sprung by winds of change,
I shiver with a restlessness. I fly.

In smoky billows, we burnish twilight
with others dangling; vesper, lark,
golden-crown and dark-eyed
junco. No rainbows to fly
over, just ribbons of amber.

I must look beyond the jet
streams, beyond weary wings.
But I miss the scientist's net,
a smudge on sunset,
then your cold hands fumbling
in razor dark. Your hands,
which know how it is to hold
a winged heart. Hands,
which question why we fly.

Will our answers ransom us? Free
again, to fly and sing arias of star-spilt
skies, of melody tripped trees,
of unmapped winds we wing?
I don't know how to call for help. Black
silence fills this blacker box. Just set me
free with hands which will write this mystery.

Pale Ride

From the cemetery I could taste
his dust in my teeth, feel the wind
give loft to my coat
to lift me to the smoldering

clouds. Found along the winding
road back, back and forth,
the palomino ran between the barn
and the pasture. Kicking up

dust, giving up silken resolution.
Once again, there was no comfort
in low church or their thin words
today. How fast the machines

go to work, planting only unrest.
But the pale ride was faster,
back and forth between barn
and pasture. And I found

the words in the cleave
of his hooves, splitting heaven's
atoms. *I should stay. No, run, run
run away with me.* Into his nostrils

he breathed the spirit of the storm. *I am free.
Here is your solace,* he said to me.

Wormholes, Vivaldi and Iris

Tracings of frost on the window
lend strange matter on a sill-
gripping day. Some are feathers,
broad enough to fan tropic fevers.

Some are toothed leaves, lacings of wood
nymphs. And some, no doubt, are wormholes,
their castings prismatic and anti-material
as the crystals that form them.

If only I could slip inside and slide
from one end, the Ice Age,
to another, a wave of purple iris
and Vivaldi's hot dark matter,

where birds are clocks—tick,
tick, flocking away. But somehow,
I get stuck inside, not enough exotic
matter to take me back or ahead,

too much doesn't matter in my blood,
too much gravity in my bed.
I am aloof to shadows on the wall,
because just as quickly shadows warp

to stranger shadows. Imagine us, physicists,
with our linear accelerators building
wormholes from hell to heaven, smirking.
Wait till the poets get their hands on this.

Dear Picasso

Ironic how Cervantes,
the docent, knows us at the museum.
Now in the gallery, I wonder how
your titles would read in another galaxy,
another time-warp. You strip "Three Graces"
of their mythology (but not of their grace).
Strange I can't remember the (dry point)
"Rape III."

>sliding down waxen leaves
>nothing to stop it
>falling . . . falling

She lingers at "Two Nude Women." In them
she recognizes your style. Did your hand
grow tired on the right side of the canvas
that you left out those lines? Not frugal
with ink for the "Repast from the Acrobat
Suites," you serve a square meal
though the diners look as hungry
as "American Gothic." Even I would undress
and dance for your flutist in red.

>Carmen dances the Habanera
>a rose in her teeth
>a cigarette in her hand

We want to ask you about your women
with their great breasts and masked
and faceless pinball heads. Are we so small
and so grotesque? Do you paint

the stuff of nightmares or just under radar
thought that we should cause such distress?
But how you aggrandize the Minotaur and taunt
the blind, tilting at "Don Quixote"
in emerald and ruby of a vast mind.

        if only my words
        BE GIANTS too
        I am dreaming... dreaming

Talk Me Down

Don't talk bohemian to me.
Speak in tongues. Of Greek,
Aramaic and Romany, of life
on the road chasing stars,
of anti-gravity and smoky bars.

Don't talk inanities to me.
Talk dirty. Of tapping roots
in velvet earth and wrapping
fine tendrils around my hair,
of showering me in fronds
of ferns, of twisting me
with lightning's F-5 fix.
Don't wine and rose me. Talk
dirty with fire to cinder speed.

Don't talk sense to me. Of
IRA's, berry patch and doing
lunch. Speak to me of beauty.
Eyes that gleam, ears that turn,
souls that fly. Talk of violet-
sprung ruins, raiments of moss
and lichens, thunderstorm cliffs
and lightning riffs. Talk pretty.

Don't talk war to me. Holy, petty
or otherwise. Don't talk of killing
or other bloody alibis. Speak to me
dolce. In the key of G. I will ride
that melody until the day I die.

Cold Lies on Hot Jupiters

Mind the ecology of bohemians on Hot
Jupiters for burnished niche of Icarus
is their cold lie, where solar flares are too
close to call and slow, steady burns climax

successions. Their system, unstable
at best, compels them to prey on fast
comets and trendy protoplasm, while they
drink absolute alcohol on a methane beach,

watching triple sunsets that last
thirty-three days, waiting for triple
sunrise when they'll hitchhike away
to an orbit of graver gravity.

Never mind those creatures
who brave the insult of the Great
Red Spot and sacrifice to feed volcanoes
on Io, dancing in place at the bottom

of the food chain, beneath Europa,
Calisto and Ganymede. Too tired
to be inspired, too inflamed to crash
orbit, too awake to ignore the Horsehead

Nebula in their bed. Here I stand, too
grounded to speak the truth, a noisy speck
of dust, a seeker of sixth magnitude,
almost invisible in my cold lies.

Crows in a Cornfield

Summer, winter or fall,
we think next season
we can do it over, amend
broken words. Next season
we will find redemption, we will
find the words, the incendiary
thoughts, the cure, the fix.

And I am in that cloudy
place at the bottom
of a glass. Been here
for days and restless
nights, waiting for walking
dreams that never last. I wait
for roosting crows to sing
their rough lullabies, to murder
days marching in, never
knowing if they'll show.

I call them.

One with black eyes. One
with blue. One to see. One
to speak with gilded tongue.
One to know. One to divine.
One to spell clouds passing by.

And they land, soft powder
and flurry. One by one,
they land. One to soothe,
one to mediate. Soft, so soft,

to forgive. Silent hold
to redeem from bruised clouds.
They weave their black magic
over me. One for hours,
one for pretty lies, one
to perch over me
to close my far-sighted eyes.

Handle with Care

The blush tulips on the table
are turning out, explicitly curling
around their hothouse sex. And I
think they are more strange
and velvet now than in crystal
vase. I refrain from touching
them in this fragile state for fear
I would drain them of their pearl
petals destined for coarse oak

grain. And if I pick raspberries,
I must take care for a slip
of the wrist will unravel the fruit
twisting it from the vine. If I
serve red wine, I must release
the cork without a trace and let it
breathe to unlace its torpidity. You

come without warning labels,
without alarms, bite, sting, fallout
or screams. I must handle you
with care. Treat you like a found
cobra's egg and unleash you like
a fledgling raven. Lay you in a nest
of mink scorpions and tether you
with satin lizard garrote. I must

be so gentle with you, serving you
lotus and absinthe, enough to keep
you languorous and happy but barely
breathing.

Dr. Marvel's Magical Medicinals

Les Merveilles de Quatre Saisons—
the sign on my wagon sells my good,
spring, summer, winter or fall,
I have a cure for every reason. I call—
                I've got pills for every ache
                or ill. Nitrate of Sanguinaria
                for a stomach full of butterflies
                or Sentellaria for a wicked hysteria.
                Try this tincture of honey bee
                for a seven-year itch or ten drops
                of ether on a lump of sugar
                if your smile's but a crooked twitch.
With my wagon hitched to my star-
marked mare, I hustle from Holland
to Peru, from Crab Orchard to Elk Creek.
Within five day's ride, I am legend. I cajole—
                Step up quick, sir,
                for a dram of this elixir
                if your bones are feeling heavy
                as a ten-foot blizzard.
                When you're in a bind or fix,
                there's Echinacea for dullness
                of your intellect. And folks, that's gonna
                slow you down, no leaps, no bounds.
When you've got questions
I'll just knit my brows or your son's
leg as a favor. I make sound predictions
as to your welfare or behavior. I conjure—
                And folks, I'm not gonna tell you
                twice, when you're feeling dragged
                backwards, Ignatia works very nice.

And a potion of ergot will get your ticker
going or turn you into a werewolf,
lest I forgot. Take passionflower
as a soporific, before long, your dreams
will look terrific. There's tincture of thyme
for the gloom. Deadly nightshade
for hebetude. Just take your pick,
when you haven't got that get-up-and-go attitude.
Come, one, come all to Dr. Marvel's medicine show.
I'll take you up when you're feeling low.

Flat Out Doing Sixty

FINES DOUBLE
NEXT FIVE MILES

They minded this sign for no reason.

PRISON AREA
HITCHHIKING
PROHIBITED

But they missed this one just past the Elko
Conoco. Rafe and Shelly, they was guided
by voices, not signs, and a water-cooled
engine. They must've heard demons the day
they picked me up, the man in red
with dark orgies in his eyes, the man
with no name and everyone else

to blame, who troubles the knife in his pocket,
and who'd have no trouble killing them
just for their VW if only they didn't
pull off every few miles, pull out shovels,
and bury road kill like cousins, tears
and tiny crosses for Mother Earth to mourn
but it wasn't just her loss, they said.

This is too fucking messy, I think. Their bodies
would just add to the roadside litter. Guess I need
a new hobby. My arms are mapped with rude
tattoos and my cell mate's been mapped up
pretty good, too. I'm bored and I'm itchy

and now that I'm out, there ain't nothing to do.
Damn them, they shoulda taken Route 22.

Dog Star Rising

Now is the time to call
seed merchants liars while you
compare page-two white sunflowers
with your rangy yellow ones.
Time when crows are just
blackboard scratches against
a schoolboy's sky. Now
is the time and time again
when dog days of August reign,
time when the sun drags the haze
like a scythe, when even Sirius
winces at sunrise. Now is the time
for creatures alive to show
their blue colors before they fall
into disguise. Before their demise,
cicada song rustles corn stalks like
raccoon claws and passion, passion . . .
I stammer, passionflowers bloom.

>   once upon a caterpillar
>   once upon a vine
>   there lays black swallowtail
>   when will he be mine?

Dog daze of August when intention
pools around you like hot candle wax
and you know this must be the greenest,
sweetest blush of sweat and tender harvest.

once upon a moonflower
once upon a crime
I will taste your mortal petals
kiss me when it's time.

Without a Net

Spotlights shine on Carmello
in the center ring, saber to the teeth,
chalked hands and slippered feet,
gripping a ladder of faith to the wire
just a breath below the big top. No one
laughs at the clowns once I, Fausto,
tell the roustabouts to pull away the net.

Then, I nod to my brother, Dominico,
bum a smoke from my brother, Mario,
and slip out through a back tent flap.
As I wave to the side-show hawkers,
I beg a light from Freydo, the fire-eater,
and slither past Volante, snake-charmer,
and Stephano, seven digit sword-swallower.

A corona of white defines Carmello
in his red satin, cinched with sequins,
as he waves, fists clinched, to eyes in the dark.
The crowd, it roars like tigers in the next
ring and pouts its red-caked smiles
at the absurd saber. (Didn't I warn of the tug
of fear and the downdraft of doubt?)

Beneath a night tainted red,
I rush town streets to meet a girl
from there, who waits for me
against the brick wall of the pharmacy,
where ivy grows from a frown in the wall.

Once we meet, even crowned in circus
lights, no one could defuse wind from want.

The girl hears good-byes in my gasps
of hello, my reckless cries and wordless
sighs. Still in the pulse of fevered stars, the strike
of a match stirs torch to lips, spark to thigh.
The tangle of night's ivy burnishes us
into one trick knot of illusion, tarnished
by one shudder when I hear the crowd shriek.

Heart aching, I run to striped tents, only after
they send in the clowns who enshroud,
with their stilted, grease paint smiles,
the twisted spider silhouette of Carmello,
cast in sawdust of my abandon. The crowd
only chants, where is the bread? I curse the day
I was born and the dark one with the pagliacci smile.

Looking Glass Menagerie

It is the way of beasts,
the wicking of air, holding
on tongues the taste of sulfur,
the taste of nightshade or sweet grass,

the taste of blood. Though what they
don't grasp in their non-opposable
paws, they breathe in
the noble air of angels. Dumb,

not dumb, their rasping or forked
tongues taste honey, lightning,
taste a wind gone foul but never
evil. When words fail us,

instinct does not fail them. When
there are no words, impulse builds
on impulse, snarls stand on growls
in this glassy eye carousel of beasts,

looking glass menagerie where elephants
know where and when to lay down
their bones. And chimps glimpse
some Paleolithic sense of future, making

tools. That frail steeled flight
of sparrows and monarchs, mile
after thin mile of day or night. Is it
just behavior or some kind of direct
connect with the gods? By Darwin,
they mate only to procreate

the fittest and nurture by numbers.
We mate/marry with nods to love,

with banns of proximity. Like black
stars of Abell 44, consuming mirror images,
never comprehending the like love throes
of black widow spiders,
never devouring millions of stars.

Road Undertaken

I-80 moves along, not me. I-80,
where the road and your breath
are sucked out the exhaust and there's
no turning back, where barbed wire
holds in nothing but tumbleweeds
and fear, where you are taking coup
by scalping sagebrush with your glare
till you're sick of the motion
and backpack commotion and side roads
scribed by the risky slipstream
of a Dodge truck. I restart the wrecking
ball thunder of Zeppelin for the hundredth
time, while curved edges of clouds feather
out with rain that falls like a cheap
beaded curtain over a tractor tilling
dust along a road, where people write
pride and love on mountains, where
mountains write the sky. Nothing
lives at Hot Springs but watery
ghosts yet the glitter dirt pleads
gold. In North Valmy, monsters
on the high plains shoot wires and smoke
across the road while I stare
through a windshield of gut intention
to a view, which develops like a sepia
photograph. I have so much
to do, I think, speeding Coal Canyon,
where factories spew out more regret
than remorse and in Kimball, where mile
markers are manly mirages marking
eternity like the pigs-in-a-blanket

in Mustang but then I haven't eaten
since Lamb's Canyon. A rainbow
of laurels dangles over my head by Kearney
but I am too sick to notice, sick of all
the things I've missed, sick of the whine
the road can't fix. Catatonia is survival
on the road, the road whose name
and color I may never know.

Crow

Eyes black as blood
is red, no rose-colored
lenses impede my view
as we sift through a copse
of yellow trees. Sight
is once, twice second sight.
I see that which blinds you;
the glitter, the grisly,
the glamour, the graveyard.
Set your clocks by me. I toll
the darkest hour. My range
is dominion for I am touched
like Black Elk and cursed
says I. I speak in cause
and effect but you only
hear the cause. I fly high
octane ether and roost
in netherworlds. Hollows
of my bones are filled
with chants and faraway voices.
Find no tricks, no didactic
speech. Listen to my caws.
Take heed of my screech.

Heart of MCG-8-22-15
(Art and Science of Black Stars and Blue Poets)

Some energy barely escapes
your afternoon watch and shifts
red off me, spinning from the event
horizon of your dark star pull
and I wonder why those telescopes
peer so seriously. I must remember,
as I watch over a choir of crows,
singing adagios, it's all relativity.

Pardon me if it's something I say,
I don't really know the adept
way to get to the heart of things. Before
even approaching light speed, I
may be thrust, along with apple peels
and egg shells, through Occam's
gruesome blades of your grave
singularity. On paper it's all relativity.

Leaving only a trail of photon crumbs,
dressed in space-time fabric, a quest
begins to dig up a poet's bones. Time
to ask the Homeric question but I can't
relate so I'm slipping fast and this watch
won't last forever. Then the digger tells
me, those bones are not Homer's, just sacrificed
offerings. In faith, it's voodoo relativity.

Thursdays on Meadow Road

This ain't no chain of daisies
I'm doing. Yellow letters, lettuce
leaves and cat crap chase the truck
like seagulls flapping over a delta
barge. I'd rather be hauling ass
back to Corpus Christi than hauling
trash for you. I run four more cans
to the truck, thinking this is only
temporary but for now I see
your dirt. I know what you do
with that half-drunk champagne,
day-old shrimp, those dirty check
stubs and empty vials. I see what you
do in the night. Garbage in,
garbage out. I'm too young
for this shit, especially on sunny
days when I wear sweat like basting
and flies like honey. And even
when I ride upwind, three bars
of soap won't get me a girl. Nicest
thing ever done for me was last
summer, Thursdays on Meadow Road,
and this old lady snuck us cold beer
wrapped up in paper bags. Guess
she moved or something. Shit,
this is only temporary. And the best
it gets is when I climb on shotgun
and Pete takes a turn real fast and I
chill out when the wind hits
my face, when gulls fly, when
I could be anything.

Branta Canadensis

Ancient, the elements rule.
Abide by water as by earth
but there is only one breath-
taking rush—by air.
Under waxing Snow Moon's
light, I breathe easy—
in for upstroke of wings,
out for downstroke of wings.

I soar between ermine clouds
and memory of sky-eating
lights. Flight feathers dull
to gray, I look down on watchers
who watch me straggle behind
this gaggle, riding slipstream,
ghosting comet's miss, that stardust
kiss, those shadow puzzles
of green and black, that copper
leaf-strewn watery wrinkle

pointing north. I ride
the current of flock, of legion,
of storybook. One more breath,
one more stroke. Northward, I fly
no other direction but home.

Seasons and Memory

Scratch of lightning on tinderbox
birch, the way of seasons and memory.

When the land is steeped
and rolling with tender sage,
I can hardly remember
fall's dry, yellow winds.

And when winter drags white
wasteland, abandoned silence,
devoid of fire and hope, I can
hardly remember the fuller moons,
moss-tread barefoot nights
and painted tongues of summer.
We are revived and failing
by haunting, septic memory.

Pack frosted panes, gingerbread
and staggering tracks in the snow.
Pack rivulet streets, strawberries 'n
cream and hardening seedlings in sun.
Stow away perfumed nights, stolen
4 o'clock kiss and Hercules'
pyrotechnic dance. Pack feathered
dusk, mutant-colored maize
and incensed requiem for leaves.

Pack them all away so you won't
remember their hardships, insufferable
pleasures for we can never get enough.
If memory fails, it serves.

Celebrate your body when it's summer.
Cherish your mind when it's winter,
but live in this moment
extravagant with light.

Cathartes aura—Turkey Vulture

Ugly is as it sounds but does
no injustice to me. Companion
to beauty in its insistence. Not found
in the roadside pool or eyes
of my brothers and cousins.
Dark is dark no matter how
you paint it. I revel in repulsion
and stick with my kind for I
am purifier, tearing life
from the random disorder

of death. Dark and darker still,
I circle over scarred, unkind
land for hours, my feathers
tipping silver in the light.
My shadow looms large
then larger still, savoring,
swallowing Death whole.

From this cloud I soar
with tattered wing, vulnerable
neck, senses alert, and can
smell the dust, the dames'
rocket, the trickle of blood,
the last breath. But I am
patient and reverent before
I go to work.

At night when we roost
in this dead apple orchard,

I dream of red-dripping apples.
Restless sleep, I wonder who
will be there to bury,
to purify me. By dawn
the sorrow weighs on me so,
my wings are too heavy
for the effort of flight.

Heraldic, I pose
with night-damp wings spread,
exposed yet proud, in the sun.
Another day, still another
day's work to be done.

Friday Night Shift

Sun was sliding under doors when I climb
dusty stairs to the apartment knowing
even a shower won't get the stink
of hot steel off a me. In bed still, she's

one of them lady bugs, arms and legs stickin'
out. I kick off my boots and smell the baby
lotion she puts on her every night. She's talkin'
but I don't never get what she's saying. Hell,

when I peel off my jeans and throw 'em
in the corner, I know I ain't taking no shower
and climb into bed, too tired to be hearing
the clash of I-beams or Springsteen loops

in my head like all the shouts, whispers,
buzz of the night as I let the worries leave me,
all leave me. But then the snaps of a jacket
wake me up too soon. What the dumb-ass

deal is she doing? Saturdays she sleeps past
noon. I hear the smooth zip of her jeans
and her boot catch her foot, the static of a brush
through her hair. She's holding her breath

as she slips out to the stairs, without one sorry
word, leaving the door wide open. I can't
even open my eyes to look for her, to try
and change her mind. I'm all outta words.

Jekyll

I have been hiding it, hiding
in my parlor, in my apothecary,
in my beveled mirror for so long.
Cloaking it in fog and slogging

footsteps. No one must see
the twisted shade beneath this cover.
I try to steady myself. Tested
and tormented, I try to steady
and steel myself in my work,

that formula of redemption.
Measuring so precisely this numbing
green potion and that sickly blue
elixir, always true and steadfastly

looking, trembling to find some fix.
It must be all work. They cannot
see me this way. I am split
like a fallen tree and I can

no longer even look in puddles
in the street. It is two selves I see.
There is bad in the good and yet
still goodness in the bad. Clocks

toll this fission of two souls. Oh,
the thundering in my head. This tempest
of doubt. When will his rants quiet?
I must drink deep of this draft of red,
only perhaps to take one last gasp.

Apple Pie

Fall if you must, tumble
out of midsummer's dream
onto cold leaf-strewn floor.
Things are dying out there

and in here and I cannot
stop it. Sugar pours cool,
flour clumps warm, salt
spills to taste and luck

and shortening pulls them
together. The old highway rolls
mahogany and olive. Red tails
sift through spongy clouds

over some gasping form. Golden
wild stuff along roadsides clashes
and amends stands of sumac.
The crust rolls thin by my hands

like hundreds of times. Swollen
good-bye clouds quench
thirsts after migrants'
milo buffet. Roadside stands

have changed, taking on winds
and rain. Hard signs mark apples,
nuts, cherry wine and apple brew.
Put to the knife, apples

spin and fan in my hands.
The pie bubbles over
and we still talk of sky.

Lemon Europa

The song I play and play
while I make lemon meringue
for you, whips me back and forth
through my task, fifth gear
for the spoon. An insistent wail
through my stirring, it lays
me out cross the wood floor, bades me
amuse while I breathe sandalwood,
sugar, laurel and lemon.
The lemon curd bubbles,
then curls around the spoon
like solar flare ladyfingers.
One sustained note, one
strong hand, one tone ciphers
spoon and spine like a tuning fork.
Butter in the pan melts like flakes
of gold but sour lemon barely tempers it.
This is no veiled guitar that pillows
my hunger while I cakewalk through
the kitchen, but ravenous beetles
that gnaw on me till I am numb
and barefoot in a cold kitchen.
I wonder how many kitchens
this song has played, cakes
it has made. When the song is done,
so am I but you are gone and my lips
are left only with the taste of sage.

Roma Hands

tea leaves

Hand me your cup, my pretty. There,
the tea leaves speak of your future. Do
not fear this dragon here which tells
of sudden change for I see a bird
which tells of good news. As for the moon
and the stars? They are yours.
                              ~Vadoma

crystal gazing

To wait for the smoke is a faraway
thing. Like lightning, a cold smoke
scores the crystal. Wild, never meant
to be contained, it leeches into the room
like fire-in-the-head, disconnected,
waiting to parlay visions interrupted.
I see a thousand watchful, perfect
faces till the smoke smolders my glamour.
                              ~Keja

slave to stars

I'd rather be a Gypsy than a queen.
I'd rather be barefoot and called Tshaya
following a *vurma* of sticks and stones, drinking
coffee *sweet as heaven* and *hot as hell*
while a boy rigs a bare-backed mare we'll ride

to the next town where I'll throw cards.
I'll be *o mulo* haunting these trees,
slave to stars, a Gypsy queen down on my knees.
                              ~Tshaya

tarot

Cross my palm with silver. Ah yes,
you are cursed with impatience,
my pretty. You ask of the final
outcome. I see the approaching
vardo. The cards, they do not lie.
This I say to you, expect
the unexpected.
                              ~Tsuritsa

crystal

Enough *dukkerin'* for today, my black currant,
the stars call us now and tomorrow the road.
And I'll call the music of the spheres
for your tender ears and you will hear
strings that do not lie, guitars that cry
and castanets that will pace your heart
for the endless journey. You need not worry
about the future. The road will tell all.
Lay down, my pretty, lay down.

                              ~Djidjo

Summer Whites

Here is your list, my friend,
of frenetic ways to say good-bye
to summer. I walk from a shower
of regrets, barefoot into fall
and into summer's failing twilight,
pressing the back of my white eyelet
nightgown to bricks that hold onto heat
a little longer, storing up their fire
for the next thunder snow. And I huff
white jasmine, white moonflowers
and white four o'clocks hoping their
perfumes will ignite me and mock time
once again before I close the latched
door, which is winter. And how the whites
prevail over the darkest I planted. I
kiss them, taste them till I am wrecked
by their creeping insinuations and braid
them into my wet hair and garland them
round my damp neck. On paler skeins
of clouds, a white mask glides above trees,
teasing me with the face of a mime,
pleasing me with the face of a man.

There, nighthawk. There, incubus,
saving white mist in Andromeda, are
you the one to ransom me from winter?
Tell me your name
and I will write it, drive it, read into it,
a red abiding sun, midsummer night undone.

Last Call Bar and Dance Hall

Spend my days hauling propane
and spend my nights at this old bar
fueling my brain. The old lady's
too tired to tango no more so I chase
shots with a cold Bud with eyes peeled for
some gold-hearted whore. And the Jack
ain't got no heat even when it's poured neat.
The tunes ain't pretty even when they's sweet
as the mewl of a two-headed calf. Old Mac,
the keep, washes dishes while Ernest bends
his ear again 'bout the time Elna run off
to Elkhorn with one fast plucking poultry man.
And I talk to Mac too. Ain't much to tell.
Hell, folks say he's been deaf since ninety-two.
Ain't no one dancing no more but Lyla
and she been looking better every night,
'cause, damn, if she don't grow on you like
the green slick on a horse tank. She got
eyes like a viper and sheds like one too.
Ain't looking for no line-dancing queen,
just one who'll pull my shit-kickers off
when I fall into bed. One with more heat
in her feet than fancy thoughts in her head.
Hey, Mac, how 'bout one for the road?

Windflower Farm

West winds reign on this farm,
here in the middle of nowhere,
where I tend flowers and harvest
then sell their seeds. Not roses,

mind you, but rare fragrant ones
like Angelica, Dames'
Rocket, Moonvine, Giant
Hyacinth, and Hyssop. I am

a shy and patient man.
I watch for clouds and watch
for sun and can sort the tiniest
of seeds with a steady hand.

I am a patient farmer
when crops fail or when
customers don't buy the
white flowers of the season.

Always patient with mother,
who thought I was crazy
when I quit my job, bought
the farm and moved in

with Graham. I'm gentle
with our daughter, who would
rather skip through alyssum
than study lessons we give her.

Through all the dissent
and turmoil I remain at peace
when we bake bread incensed
with flower winds which stir

through open windows. When I
look over the fields, I'm
impatient with myself
that I can't put earth to pen and ink.
That I can't paint sky on canvas.

Golden Eagle

High in oldest hills, in moss-
lined branches of a sentient
tree, in white of innocence,
you hatch. Stimulus/response.
Your open beak compels us
to sully your down
with our bloodthirsty ways—
the taste of hare, fox and lamb.
Now I see you catch
the upwind in your tawny
feathers and watch your wings
rollercoaster with summer's
thermals and I know it is
time. Though this will be
the last time dust will shake
from this brittle tree.

I take you to the highest
spruce on this holy hill.
The wind taunts and teases
your feathers. Stimulus/
response. You edge along
the tallest limb, a high call
in your throat. You spread
your wings to their bravest lengths.
I set you free.

Briar Patch

Lay me out on twenty-two
mattresses. I'll not feel one pea
for nobility I will never be.

I could be kept so easily
on sonar, laser, radar,
honey and sassafras tea.

Rock me and roll me
over Beethoven, Brahms and Bach.
Make my alarm a metronome

for I'll never heed an atomic
clock. When I'm fat and sassy,
curse me till you're blue.

I will only sigh, taking offense
at the slightest nuance. Don't coax
me to paint-by-numbers. I need

only light. No need to spoil
me with precious gems and designer
clothes. I will still rant and invade,

a wilding field rose. Cut me
till I bleed. There will be no
need for triage for I know the point

of injury. Build me a cage
of olive branch, grape vine
and flower of moon. But never,

no never, throw me in the briar
patch. Let me root hollyhocks,
tiger lilies and Phlox of Sheep.
I need only ten karat stars where I sleep.

Remote Fishing III
Reflections upon a Visit to the Black Hills

#1
tuxedo trees, red velvet dirt, granite
hosting needy, braided blooms, mercury
glass lakes and end-of-the-rainbow
trout. this is our destination.
our intention to escape,
to drift, to band together and go
remote fishing again.

#2
while some of us must endure
the long drive, you, little one
with the moon in your eyes,
insist on riding a drugstore
bronc. it's all new to you. I hope
one day you'll ride a horse along
dusty trails. those moments
of creature plus creature—
he walks for you, he sees
for you, he breathes for you.
as I do now.

#3
where we go, you'll find no breaks
between land and sky. and here,
miles from home, there are no gaps
between the youngest and oldest
of our clan. newest to us, new
to these sleepy woods, your world
is reflected in your studied eyes.
though many arms stretch

to steady your steps, you reach
for the heritage and comfort
of Nonno's arms.

#4
after months and ages of shuffling
memories and dreams, we make
camp in a hollow on a black hill,
sentinel over sky-glittered lake. while
all of you unpack, I trail behind you
in gardens of Angel Trumpet
and nodding poppies. fire lit, I
feel the spark and burn of chill
and closeness. red-wing blackbirds
boast of possibilities. I arrive.

#5
your umbrella, slicker,
window screen, and stream
of untimely rain can't veil
your intentions for all of us—
protection, enrichment
and a smooth path. you lead
us up that pig-tail road
and when we stumble on pyrite,
you right us. we're cold, you
blanket us. fires die, you fan
them. will we on this mossy
scored land rescue you?

#6
libretto-throated birds are well noted
as they swoop while we savor
your special meal. a meal too finely
presented for blue jeans and boots.
more savory than charred hot
dogs. we don't see your face
but see your hand upon your works,
which are precious to our eyes. here
words are whispers but I scan
dreams and hopes in your smiles.

#7
rarely found in my field of view, you
scout this niche and us, its dwellers,
with macro lens and farsighted eyes,
never losing depth of field
or patience. you zoom to anatomy
of changing winds or silent walk
of deer. when you shoot black
and white, though fish-eye lens,
your images are logical yet surreal
as Escher prints. save the color
for forest's furnishings and frame
me in its leaves.

#8
foraging on flaming marshmallows
and draped chocolate, you are sustained
by undivided attention while you
focus on ducks that preen

in the settling chill that falls over
the lake, on the hiss of the campfire,
chipmunks that track your crumbs,
on nighthawk ghosts, eagle spirits.

#9
I can't spin the reel for your approving
smiles any more. though the hook
is baited with cookies and cakes,
I cast my line again with hopes to lure
you with weighted words and high
minded test. the promise of you breaks
the surface but it would take a spider's
silk to reach you in the cool depths.

#10
wilderness has imprinted its design
on us so now you explore man's
design on nature. though I drone
on, I seek to detect the eloquence
of your music and art, the reach
of your vision, your steady footsteps.
but I need only insight to understand
the nature, the strength of your love.

#11
whether you walk the streams
or chase butterflies or sugared
memories, you must prepare
to go fishing. poles need threading,
lures need feathering, silk

must be knotted and cut.
tasks must be completed
whether we fish, fish remotely
or not at all. wind in our ears,
blood in our veins, distance
in our eyes, we fish together
preparing for months and months
ages and ages.

#12
you find harmony in this echoing
lake like the backward notes
in a concerto. you tackle
the contents of that metal box
as if it held moonstone and fire
agate in black velvet. you polish
them and your world precious.
now here and so faraway, I must
capture your light-speed
thoughts, cut and polish fleeting
words in your slipstream.

#13
cell to cell, slip from slip,
you cradle him on redwood
bridge, one of many he will
cross, maybe wishing, like I do,
you could always hold him.
"why" he asks do turtles live
under bridges. breaths deep
and sure, you teach him. you

teach him why water bubbles
over the dam. who lives here
in winter. what birds with red
wings are called. where the water
goes. and how you love.

#14
yards and years away, we watch
you marching, grass to shore, never
in time to Mother Goose or nursery
rhyme, ever stepping to four-four
beat. disregarding gander's hiss,
you march to meet your newest quest.
to find in reeds quicksilver fish.

#15
night erases all color but the mystique
of this lake and the grace of you,
who are new to this road but not new
to grace. always the gentleman,
you charm seeds you sow, out-laws
and their children and gilded fishes
with your wit. you comfort
with your quiet strength, your cool
design, your acceptance and fond
good-byes. I hope the trout charm
you at sunset to fish here again.

#16
unlike cold blooded fish who nurture
by numbers, we nurture our offspring

in time, in warmth, in patience.
I try not to smother but it is
in my nature to always mother you.

#17
always preferring the background,
you found me when I was lost
and took me up those seven
little dams to climb farther
and further to score hide-and-seek
fish. it was just you and me
in a wilderness, finding each lake
more glassine and more alluring.
never catching one fish, our numbers
grow in those who are touched
by this magic and climb with us again.

#18
are poise and grace just a matter of how
bones articulate? maybe knowing
and sensing are just products
of biochemistry. nature versus nurture.
it is never enough to just see the sky.
does nature compel us to paint it,
score it, mystify it, worship it
and stretch out and reach for it?

#19
the long road, in misty backstage,
shares the scene with primal trees,
which nourish and protect saplings

with earth and clouds. here I would
frame a portrait of us. but shy, all
scatter from my view. I brush and etch
you all in with timeless colors
the wear, the wonder in your eyes,
the magic in your lives.

#20
sky, crossed and cradled by leafed-out
trees, looks the same as the view
from my front door. I am always
waiting for you, in the blaze
of sunrise or the fog of sunset. we give
you this gift of sky, this holy
air. you give us life. we will always
be waiting at the door.

#21
in this scene, our images will not
be found. only night-brushed lake
with its granite gatekeeper and electric
air. look for us in years, in beginnings,
as he takes me, this sunset, by the hand
to the lake, over rocks, through grasses,
in fading light for a last tour
of the lake like he did that first hike
up the French Creek. sense in this
reflection our victories.

#22
in fog and purple haze, I take one last
scan of this ancient land and the road,
which leads to home. in too many thin
words I have tried to express
my love for all of you, all of this.
take a breath. let it out in love songs
and dragon fire. don't let nightmares
poison your dreams. we must use
all our senses, the expanse of our minds.
we must always fish, if only remotely.

About the Author

A native of Omaha, Carla Maria Stout holds a BS in biology from Creighton University and is a master gardener, painter, star gazer, and has done research in avian physiology. Her poem "Summer Whites" was published in *The Untidy Season*, an anthology of women writers from Nebraska. She lives in Omaha, Nebraska.

www.ingramcontent.com/pod-product-compliance
Lightning Source LLC
Chambersburg PA
CBHW021449080526
44588CB00009B/762